For my amazing
Wife with all the
♡ in the world
x xx
the Finnbutt xx

By Lin-Manuel Miranda

Hamilton: The Revolution (with Jeremy McCarter)

By Jonny Sun

everyone's a aliebn when ur a aliebn too: a book

GMORNING, GNIGHT!

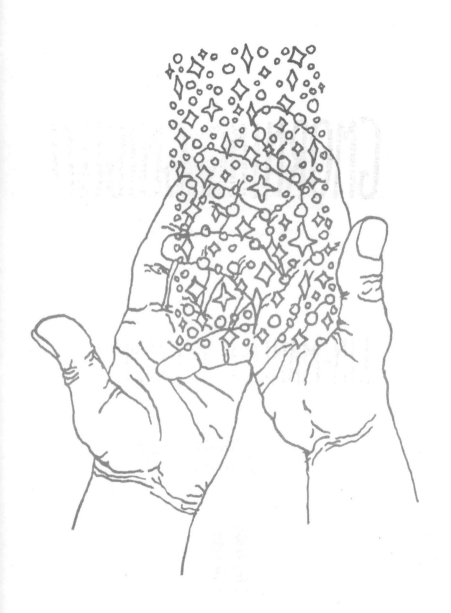

GMORNING, GNIGHT!

little pep talks for me & you

LIN-MANUEL MIRANDA

illustrated by JONNY SUN

HEADLINE

Published in the United States in 2018 by Random House,
an imprint and division of Penguin Random House LLC, New York.

First published in Great Britain in 2018
by HEADLINE PUBLISHING GROUP

4

The writings compiled in this volume originally appeared on Twitter.

Book design by Simon M. Smallman.

Cataloguing in Publication Data is available from the British Library

Hardback ISBN 978 1 4722 6281 3

Typeset in 12.84/16.6 pt Bodoni LT Pro.

Printed and bound in Great Britain by Clays Ltd, Elcograf S.p.A.

HEADLINE PUBLISHING GROUP
An Hachette UK Company
Carmelite House
50 Victoria Embankment
London
EC4Y 0DZ

www.headline.co.uk
www.hachette.co.uk

For you, holding this

introduction

I wanted to wish you good morning.
I wanted to wish you good night.
I started to write these on Twitter,
A way of just being polite.

I'm really quite hooked on the Twitter,
They should take my phone out and lock it.
The biggest distraction for someone like me?
An audience up in my pocket.

So I start the day with a greeting.
And end with a night variation.
It safeguards my evenings and weekends at home,
To sign off, a mini-vacation.

The greetings are sometimes flirtatious,
Or cheeky, or weirdly specific.
They're pulled from my life or my brain or my thoughts,
Terrific'ly Twitter prolific.

I don't have a book of quotations
Or wisdom I pull from the shelf;
Most often the greetings I wish you
Are the greetings I wish for myself.

So if I write "relax," then *I'm* nervous,
Or if I write, "cheer up," then I'm blue.
I'm writing what I wish somebody would say,
Then switching the pronoun to *you*.

And after a few years of greetings,
They started to vary in tone;
And people said, "Lin, your gmornings and nights
Are the nicest things up in my phone."

Now I get tweets like "This saved me"
Or often, "I need this reminder."
You tell me, "I printed this out and I keep it
Around, on my desk, in my binder."

So you asked, "Will you make a book, please?"
I replied, "Oh, consider it done."
Then I reached out to Kassandra Tidland
Who lit'rally RT's my best T's for fun.

And speaking of best T's, and besties,
There's besties I've made through my writing.
Among them is polymath Jonathan Sun,
His drawings and words so inviting.

Then we sat down together and made this;
It's the book that you hold in your hands.
You can open it at any moment or page
With the hope you find something that lands.

And it's nice to have things to hold on to,
Some kindness right here, within sight.
You can read this whenever you want to.
It will be here. Gmorning. Gnight.

GMORNING, GNIGHT!

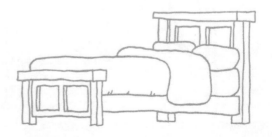

Good morning, he said.
Be at home in your head.
Make sure joy is well fed.
Don't let dread hog the bed.

Good night now, and rest.
Today was a test.
You passed it, you're past it.
Now breathe till unstressed.

Good morning, stunner.
You're just getting started.
Your age doesn't matter.
The sun is up, the day is new.
You're just getting started.

Good night, stunner.
You're just getting started.
Your age doesn't matter.
The stars are out, the night is warm.
You're just getting started.

Good morning.
Good gracious.
Your smile is
contagious.

Good night then.
Good gracious.
You're one
for the ages.

Good morning.
Lead with gratitude.
The air in your lungs, the sky above you.
Proceed from there.

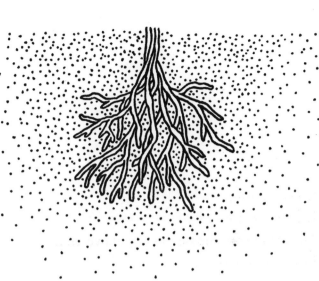

Good night.
Curl up with gratitude.
For the ground beneath you, your beating heart.
Proceed from there.

Gmorning!
You're gonna make mistakes.
You're gonna fail.
You're gonna get back up.
You're gonna break hearts.
You're gonna change minds.
You're gonna make noise.
You're gonna make music.
You're gonna be late, let's GO.

Gnight!
You're gonna fall down.
You're gonna be tested.
You're gonna learn about yourself.
You're gonna get brave.
You're gonna take stands.
You're gonna make waves.
You're gonna make history.
You're gonna need rest, REST UP.

Good morning!
Good morning!
Let's make some new mistakes!
Let's find the things worth saving in the mess our living makes!

Good night!
Good night!
Let's make some new mistakes!
Let's stumble toward success and pack some snacks
for little breaks!

Gmorning!
Before you let the world in, make
a little space for yourself.
Cup of coffee, tidy the counter,
morning quiet.
Savor the best part of that dream
you had for one more second.
Woo! Okay. Have at it, world!

Gnight!
Before you turn the world down,
make a little space for yourself.
Brush your teeth, tidy the
counter, put down the phone.
Savor the best part of the day for
one more second.
Woo! Okay. Have at it, dreams!

Good morning!
Give your time, give your heart, give your talent, give
someone something new.
It feels incredible.

Good night!
Give your time, give your heart, give your service,
give someone something you made.
It feels incredible.

Gmorning.
Check your pockets.
Got your keys?
waits
Okay, let's go!

Gnight.
Check your brain.
Got your dreams ready?
waits
Okay, let's go!

Gmorning.

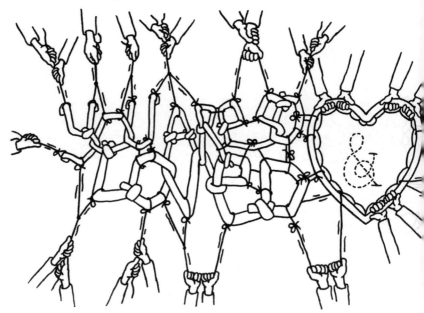

YOU ARE SO LOVED AND WE LIKE
HAVING YOU AROUND.
*ties one end of this sentence to your heart,
the other end to everyone who loves you,
even the ones you haven't heard from for a
while*
checks knots
THERE. STAY PUT, YOU.

Gnight.

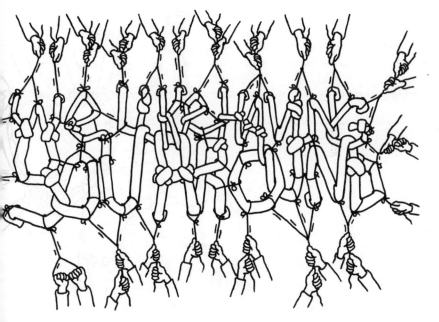

YOU ARE SO LOVED AND WE LIKE
HAVING YOU AROUND.
*ties one end of this sentence to your heart, the
   other end to everyone who loves you in this life,
   even if clouds obscure your view*
checks knots
THERE. STAY PUT, YOU.
TUG IF YOU NEED ANYTHING.

Good morning.
Keep busy while you wait for the miracle.

Good night.
Get some rest while you wait for the miracle.

Good morning, beautiful.
Make someone happy today.
I promise you it'll bounce back.

Good night, beautiful.
Make room for happiness tomorrow.
If you make room for it, it'll show up.

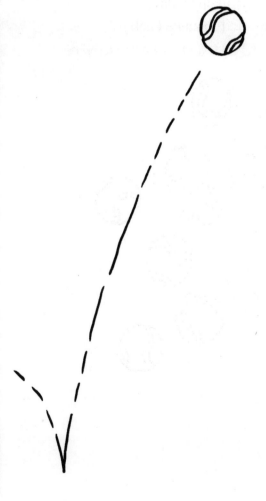

Good morning, ny, usa, world, solar system,
GALAXY, UNIVERSE, MULTIVERSE, YOU
READING THIS IN THE PALM OF YOUR HANDS.

Good night, multiverse, universe, galaxy,
solar system, world, usa, ny, YOU and your
cells, molecules, atoms, electrons, quarks.

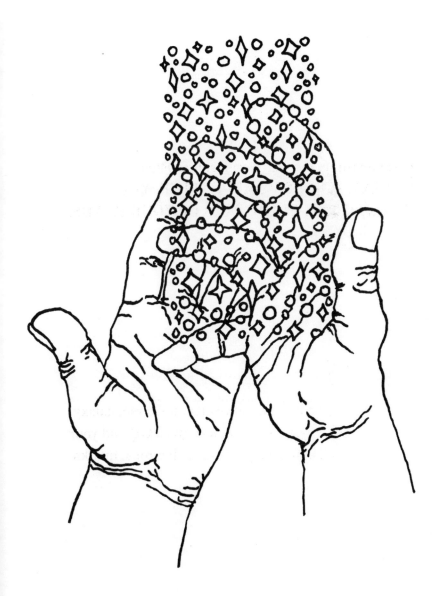

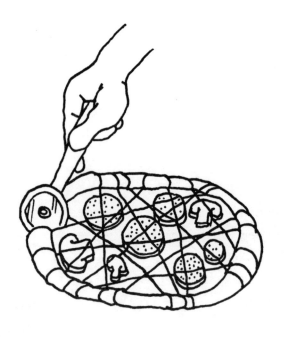

Gmorning!
Woke up achy and sad? Not alone.
Woke up with purpose and joy? Not alone.
Any way you slice it, you're not alone.
Let's go.

Gnight!
Headed to bed achy and sad? Not alone.
Headed to bed with gratitude and
satisfaction? Not alone.
Any way you slice it, you're not alone.
Let's zzzzzzzzzz.

Good morning! Face the day! If the day
looms too large, kick it in the shins so
it has to face you!

Good night. Way to face the day.
Now climb into bed with the night
and draw the shades.

Gmorning!
*quietly confident in the manifold gifts you possess,
  both known and unknown to you*
Right behind you.
You got this.

Gnight!
*over here marveling at your manifold gifts and just
  how bright you shine, every day*
Trust your gut.
Dream big.

Gmorning!
The moment that connects you to your true passion
might be on the other side of breakfast.
Or just a baby step there.
Let's see!

Gnight!
The moment that connects you to your true passion
might be on the other side of tonight.
Or just a baby step there.
Let's see!

Gmorning.
Relax your shoulders.
Gah, you didn't realize they were all tensed up,
did you?
Me neither!
Okay, let's go.

Gnight.
Relax those shoulders.
The day makes 'em seize up on all of us.
Oof. Get some rest.
Okay, sleep easy.

Good morning, you magnificent slice of perfection.
Yeah, you.

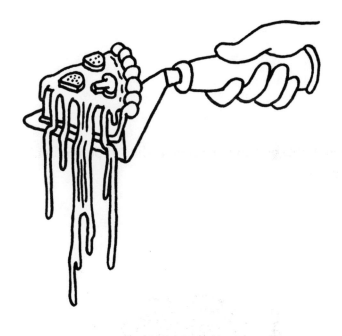

Good night, you generous helping of
flawlessness. I'M LOOKING AT YOU.

Good morning! Wear
sensible shoes as you
kick down doors!
Whoopshh!

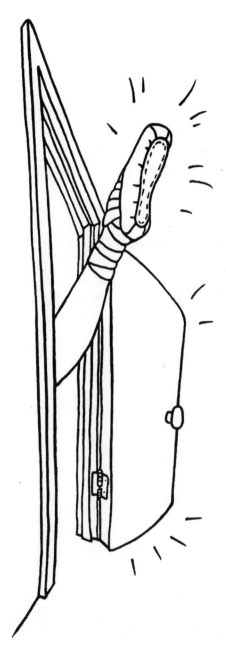

Good night! Take off your sensible shoes, put on your dancin' shoes, you deserve it.

Good morning.
Everything could change today.
Or one tiny, vital thing.
What it WON'T be is a rerun of yesterday.
Let's see.

Good night.
Everything could change tomorrow.
Or one tiny, vital thing.
What it WON'T be is a rerun of today.
Rest up.

Gmorning, love.
Your best impulse, that selfless impulse, let
it take the wheel.
Let it drive you toward the person you
dreamed you'd be.

Gnight, love.
That need to rest, that constructive impulse, let
it take the lead.
I hope you dream the best, coolest shit. Let's go.

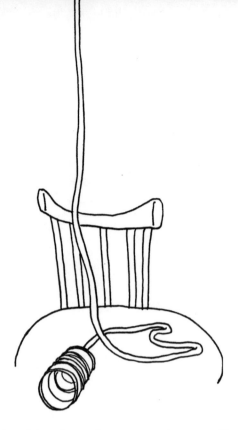

Call that friend you keep meaning to call, despite the time that's piled up. Pride is dumb. They miss you too. Good morning!

Good night. Hope you called that friend of yours!

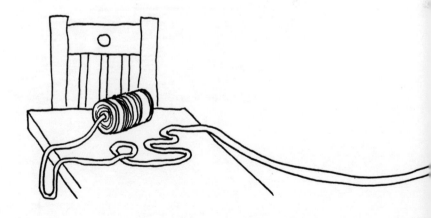

Gmorning.

Breathe deep.

That hitch in your breath is a record scratch.

That throbbing in your temple is the bass, and you control the volume knob.

The scars in your mind and your heart are grooves that run deep.

YOUR music. YOUR heart. YOUR life.

You got the aux cord.

Bump it.

Gnight.
You got the aux cord.
Your mind is your own.
Your heart is your own.
You set the playlist.
Bump it.

Good morning!
When you were born you held infinite promise.
You're older, you're all banged up by life,
But you hold that promise still.

Good night!
When you were born you held infinite promise.
You're older, you're all banged up by life,
But you hold that promise still.
KEEP GOING.

GMORNING.

Grateful for the very NOTION of you, even more grateful for the reality.

Look at you, a dream realized.

We're off! Let's go!

GNIGHT.

Grateful for the REALITY of you, even more grateful for the notion of tomorrow.

Rest up. We need you at your best.

Good morning.
Sometimes staying under the covers
seems like the best option.
I feel you.
But cmon, let's go see
what's out there.

And there is your comfy bed,
right where you left it.
You earned this good rest.
Good night.

Good morning, you Matryoshka dolls,
you carry so many versions of yourself
around inside you.
Take a seat, chill for a minute.

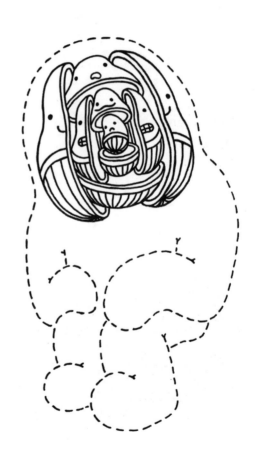

Good night, you Matryoshka dolls,
stack 'em up and pack 'em in.
You contain multitudes.

Good morning.
Take a breath.
Then another.
Repeat.
Move at your pace.
You got this.

Good night.
Take a breath.
Then another.
Repeat.
Shake off the day.
Sweet dreams.

Gmorning, friendos!
Make good choices!
Listen to your
inside voices!

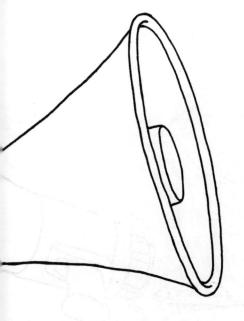

Gnight, friendos!
Make good choices!
Live your life
and raise your voices!

Gmorning.
I don't know how to tell you this,
but
you're not perfect.
You never will be.
You keep growing and messing up
and learning,
and your quirks become strengths.
You are SO much better than
perfect, love.

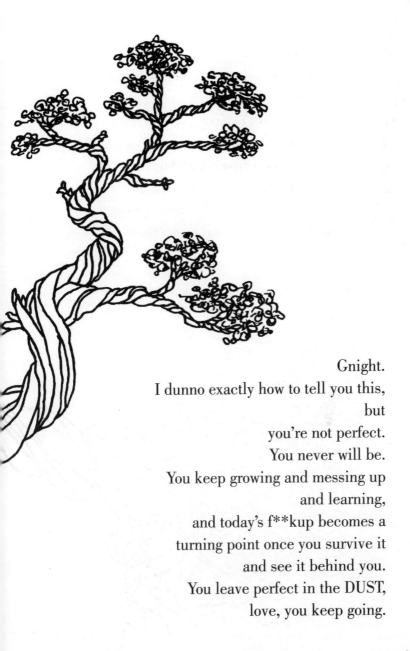

Gnight.
I dunno exactly how to tell you this,
but
you're not perfect.
You never will be.
You keep growing and messing up
and learning,
and today's f**kup becomes a
turning point once you survive it
and see it behind you.
You leave perfect in the DUST,
love, you keep going.

Gmorning.
Crawl before you walk before you run before you fly
before you ASCEND TO GREATNESS
& get some food in you, maybe a banana.
Vamos!

Gnight.
Brush your teeth before you sleep before you dream
before you fly before you CHANGE THE WORLD.
And stay hydrated!

Good morning.
You've been playing this open-world game for a
while now.
Complete a mission today.
Gain some new powers.

Good night, kids.
Level up.

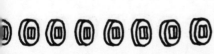

Good morning, you.
It's been a minute.
smiles
MY FRIEND LIKES YOU.
runs away

Good night, you.
It's been a minute.
walks away, shouts over shoulder
THE FRIEND WAS ME, I'M THE FRIEND.
runs out of sight

Gmorning!
I wish you clarity today.
Clarity of thought, clarity of expression, and a direct
line between what you feel and what to do about it.

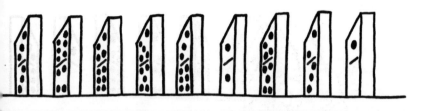

Gnight!
I wish you clarity tonight.
Clarity of self, clarity of purpose, and a direct line
between who you want to be and how to get there.

Things may never be like this again.
That could be good news or bad news
to you, but it's true nonetheless.
Gmorning.

Everything is changing all the time.
May as well lean into it.
Gnight!

Good morning!
Get after what you want.
Leave excuses on the side of the road.
Don't you feel lighter?

Good night.
We're closer than where we started.
Nothing but open road ahead.
Let's go!

Gmorning!
Write a bit, just for yourself.
Give that maelstrom in your head a place to land.
Look at everything swirling around in there!

Write some thoughts down for yourself.
Grab what you can, pin it to the page.
Look at that! How long you been hanging on to those?
Gnight!

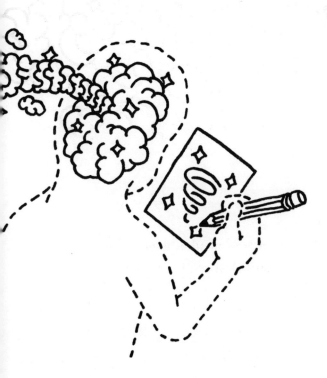

Peep the pep in your step
and the glide in your stride.
You're a knockout, my friend.
Let yourself be your guide.
Gmorning!

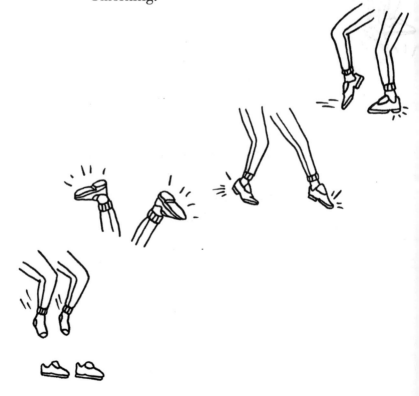

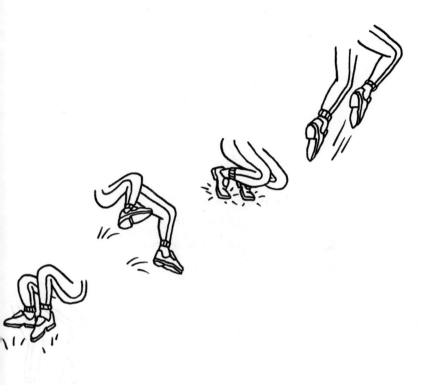

Jaws will drop as you bop,
catch your eye passing by.
You're a knockout, my friend.
Be yourself, let it fly.
Gnight!

Gmorning.

You've got stuff in your head that no one else has got.
And you've got stuff in your head that you think you
bear alone, but I PROMISE you share with so many.
Only way to know the difference is to spill it out.
On paper, into a mic, to a shrink, onto a canvas.
Let's go!

Gnight.
Rest your gifts,
rest your burdens,
rest your secrets,
rest your dreams,
rest your unrequited loves, rest the loves that
sustain you.
Tomorrow you can harvest them all again.
On paper, into a mic, to a shrink, onto a canvas.
For now, rest.

You're so pretty I can't look directly at you.
You're an eclipse.
Good morning.

The sun is gone but you remain,
undimmed and glorious.
Good night.

HAVE A GOOD MORNING NO PRESSURE
THOUGH

HAVE A GOOD NIGHT EVERYONE IS
COUNTING ON YOU
SWEET DREAMS

Good morning.
I'm tired. I bet you're tired.
But we're awake and alive and that's enough. Cmon.
Cmon.

Good night.
I'm tired. I bet you're tired.
But we're awake and alive and that's enough. Cmon.
Cmon.

Gmorning.
Inertia's a helluva drug.
If you've been going nonstop,
be an object at rest.
If you've been at rest too long,
get in motion.
Don't rely on an external force,
kick inertia in the grundle, let's GO.

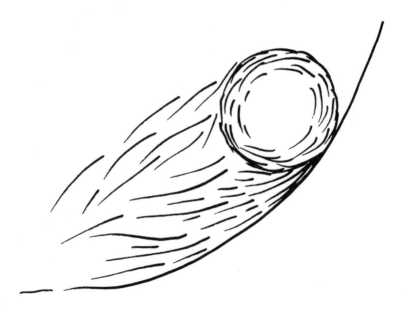

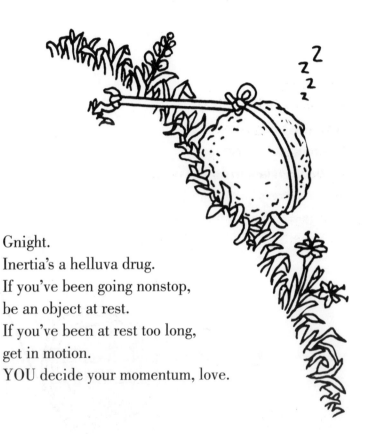

Gnight.
Inertia's a helluva drug.
If you've been going nonstop,
be an object at rest.
If you've been at rest too long,
get in motion.
YOU decide your momentum, love.

Gmorning!
Your mind is yours alone.
Do what it takes to make yourself comfy.
Build a library in there, play some music.
Make it your home.

Gnight!
Your mind is yours alone.
Do what it takes to make yourself comfy.
Draw the blinds, kick out unwelcome guests.
Make it your home.

Good morning!
*engages in complicated
   handshake that injures us both*
Ow! Worth it! Go get 'em!

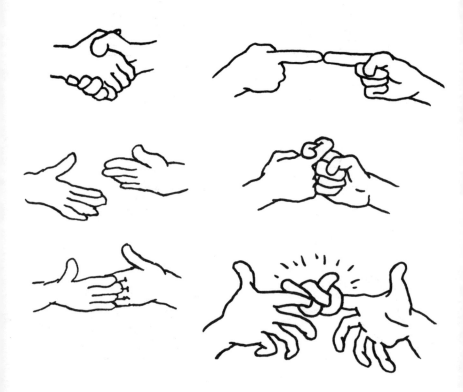

Good night!
*engages in complicated handshake that
  injures us both*
Oops! Put ice on that! Get some rest!

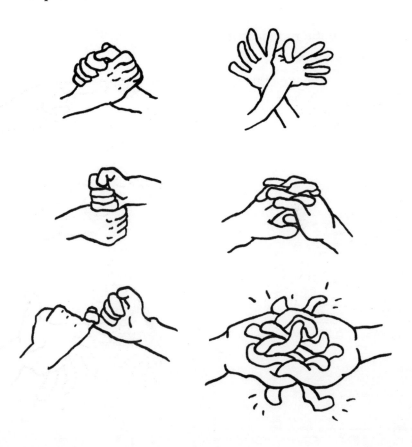

Gmorning.
In your corner,
even in the roundest of rooms.
On your side,
even if it makes this seesaw kind of boring.

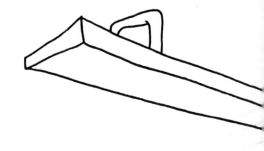

Gnight.
Holding your hand,
even if it's sticky from jelly or honey.
On your team,
even when you're playing solitaire.

The world changes.
The ground shifts.
We still make plans.
We still find gifts.
Gmorning.

The world changes.
The earth spins.
We grieve our losses.
We eke out wins.
Gnight.

Good morning.
Put some music in someone else's life today.
Make the world a mixtape and see what it gives
you in return.

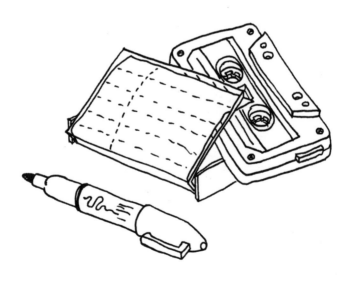

Good night.
Put some music in your life tonight.
Make yourself a mixtape and see where
your heart goes.

stands at roulette table
Gmorning!
pushes all the chips in your direction
I'm betting on YOU.
Dealer: Sir, that's not how this works—

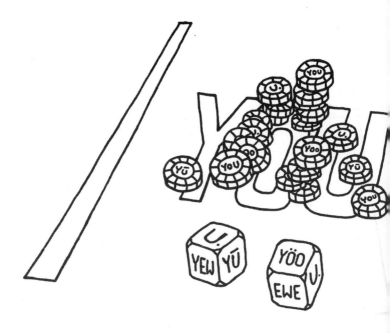

stands at the craps table
Gnight!
rolls dice
I'm rolling the dice on YOU.
begins singing "Luck Be a Lady"
Dealer: Sir, are you playing or—

Good morning.
Your pace today.
No one else's.
You can't be rushed, you can't be slowed down.

Good night.
Your pace in this life.
No one else's.
You can't be rushed, you can't be slowed down.

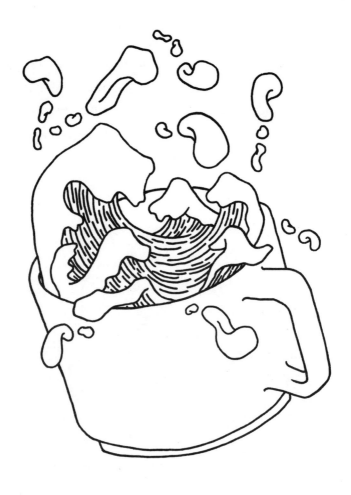

Good morning.
Woke up grateful for the air
in my lungs, the sleep in my eyes,
the ache in my bones,
the chance to say hello again.

Good night.
Lying down grateful for the air
in my lungs, the sleep in my eyes,
the ache in my bones,
the chance to see you tomorrow.

Gmorning.

Untie just ONE of the knots in your stomach.

Cross ONE thing off your list.

Call ONE loved one and surprise them with some kindness.

Damn, look at all the ROOM YOU MADE FOR SOMETHING NEW, KID.

Gnight.

There are still knots in your stomach.

Mine too.

A good night's rest won't undo them completely, but it loosens their grip and softens the strands.

Close your eyes and
MAKE ROOM FOR SOMETHING NEW, KID.

Good morning.
You are stunning.
Use your power wisely.

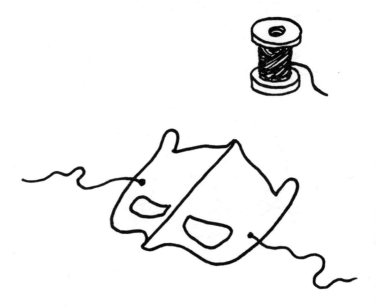

Good night.
You are stunning.
Lay down your burdens.

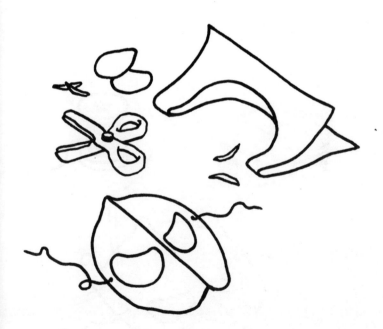

Gmorning.

You've had too many apps open for too long.

Close your eyes.

Check all systems.

Soft reboot.

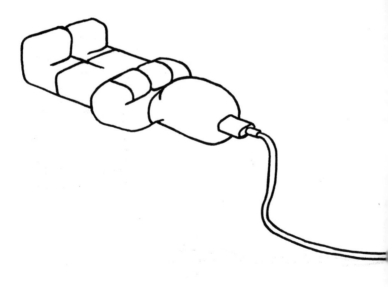

Gnight.
Don't wait until low power mode.
Close your eyes.
Close all unnecessary apps.
Recharge.

Good morning!
Rise and shine!
or
Rise and sulk!
or
Rise and weep!
or
Rise and roar!
but
RISE.

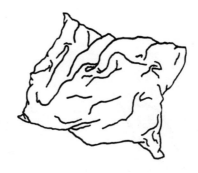

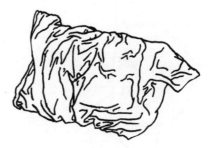

Good night!
Rest and relax!
or
Rest and rejoice!
or
Rest and rejuvenate!
or
Rest and redouble your efforts!
but
REST.

Good morning.
Keep going.
They will move the goalposts.
They will upend the board when they're in check.
Life WILL be unfair.
YOU keep going.

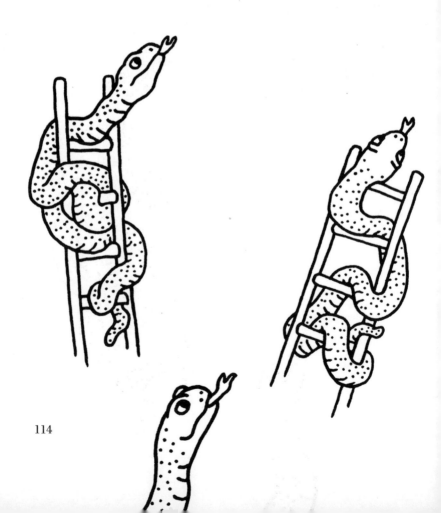

Good night.
Keep going.
They will change the rules on you.
There will be chutes lurking after ladders.
Life's not fair.
YOU keep going.

Good morning.
I believe in you.
Not always in our leaders,
not always in the subway schedules,
but always in you.
You, unwavering.

Good night.
I believe in you.
Not always in our institutions,
not always in my own strength,
but always in you.
You, evergreen.

Good morning!
You were lucky enough to wake up today, so cmon.
Socks before shoes, let's go.

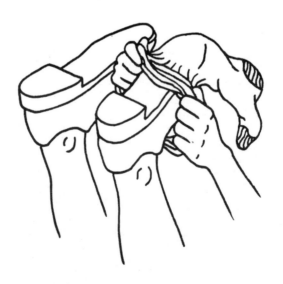

Good night.
You were lucky enough to make it through today, so take it easy.
Brush your teeth, *a dormir*, let's go.

Gmorning!
This first school dance in the gym is hella scary
but good music is playing,
and your friends are here,
so f*** it, let's DANCE.

Gnight!
The first school dance in the gym is hella scary,
it's dark in here,
but the music is loud
and we'll never be this young again, let's DANCE.

Gmorning. Bring it in. Group hug. Okay.
Proceed.

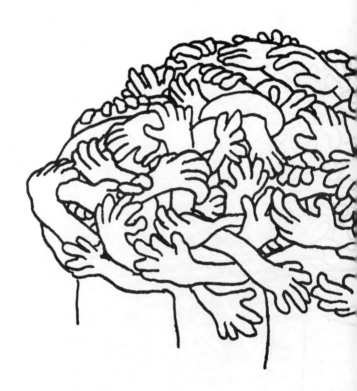

Gnight, guys. One more group hug. *Ast.*
Get some sleep.

Good morning.
You got a good head on your shoulders.
As for your shoulders?
F***ing magnificent.
GO get 'em today.

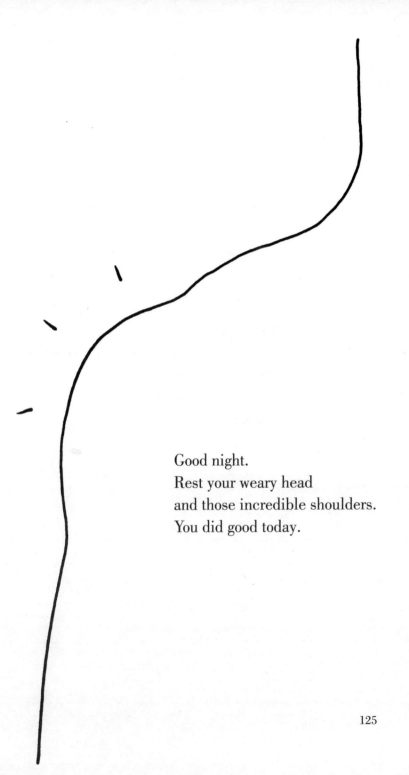

Good night.
Rest your weary head
and those incredible shoulders.
You did good today.

Good morning.
Dubious.
But doing this.

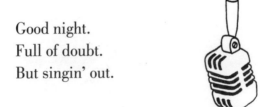

Good night.
Full of doubt.
But singin' out.

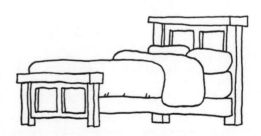

Gmorning.
Your worst fears about yourself only need a drop of
attention and sunlight to grow quick and wreck your
whole shit.
Clear away those weeds.
Take time to harvest your strengths and your joys.
Water and sunlight to the best in you.

Gnight.
Doubts may grow as shadows loom,
when you're alone with your thoughts.
Plant music, art, pics of the ones you love
in the darkest corners.
Harvest the fruits of your daydreams and rest.
Water and sunlight to the best in you.

Good morning.
Your very presence is intoxicating.

Good night.
Your very absence is sobering.

Good morning.
Side kick your fears.
Front kick your distractions.
Boom! You go up a belt!

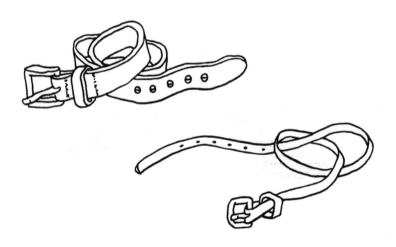

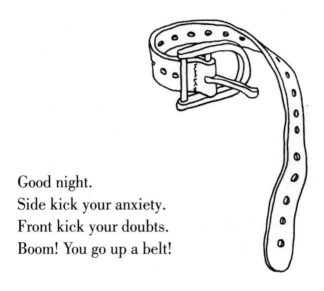

Good night.
Side kick your anxiety.
Front kick your doubts.
Boom! You go up a belt!

Gmorning.
Look at you!
The miracle of you, the thrill of you
becoming who you'll be!
spits, wipes your cheek
Just a little shmutz, got it.
Okay, stunner, GO, they ain't ready for you!

Gnight.
Look at you!
The miracle of you, the thrill of you
becoming who you'll be!
tousles your hair
Okay, stunner, REST UP, save some of that perfect for
tomorrow.

Gmorning!
No exact recipe for today.
Gather all available ingredients and whip yourself up
something delicious.

Gnight.

You whipped up a great day out of all available ingredients!

Feast on the leftovers, reminisce. Enjoy where you've been.

Gmorning!
Use your brains,
use your heart,
use your courage.
And click those heels if you need to peace out!

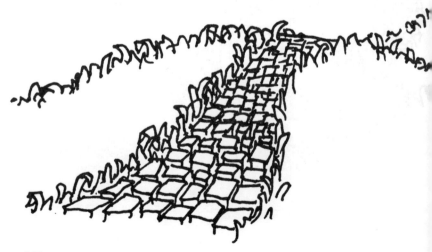

Gnight!
clicks heels three times

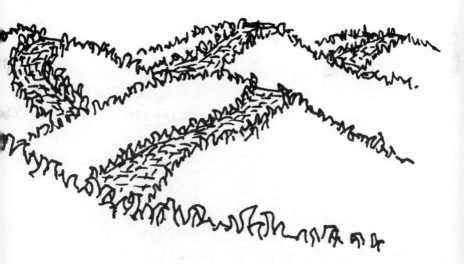

Gmorning.
This feeling will pass.
This workload will pass.
These people will pass.
But look at you, with the gift of memory.
You can time travel to the good stuff just by
closing your eyes & breathing.
Then come right back to now, eyes up for
the good stuff ahead.
You magic thing.

Gnight.
This moment will pass.
This fatigue will pass.
Tonight will pass.
But look at you, with the gift of imagination.
You can teleport to where you're happiest just by
closing your eyes & breathing.
Then come right back to now, check in with
the present.
You magic thing, you.

Gmorning from the younger version of you,
who couldn't wait to be you at this age right now.

Gnight from the older version of you,
who remembers the very moment you are in right now
and is grinning from ear to ear, because
you have no idea about
the wonders ahead.

You're indescribable.

We writers spend our lives trying to do you justice.

And you're always more than we can capture.

Good morning.

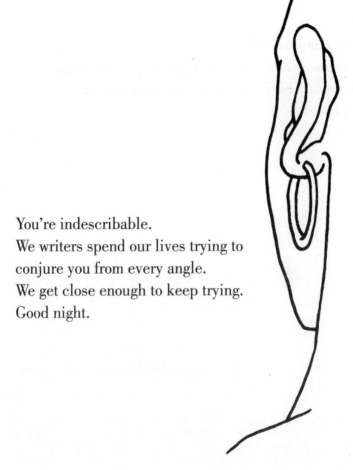

You're indescribable.
We writers spend our lives trying to
conjure you from every angle.
We get close enough to keep trying.
Good night.

Good morning.
Eyes up.
Hearts up.
Minds sharp.
Compassion on full blast.
sips coffee
Okay, let's go.

Good night.
Eyes shut.
Hearts open.
Minds calm.
Empathy on full blast.
sips tea
Okay, let's go.

Gmorning.
Sometimes there are garbage trucks
blocking every road.
They're doing their job and so are you.
Peace to the garbage trucks and the folks
just doing their jobs,
peace to a world that sometimes
puts us at cross purposes,
and peace to you, on your way,
for as long as it takes.

Gnight.
Sometimes there's traffic in every lane,
a galaxy of folks moving in the same direction.
Peace to the kids asleep in backseats,
peace to the miracles of merging lanes, wherein we
inch forward and learn to let each other in,
and peace and patience to you, on your way home.

Awaken ancient forms and play within them,
Sift gold amidst the wreckage of your slumber;
Renew your passions, maybe Pinterest pin them,
Tell that one toxic friend, "Yo, lose my number."
The day is clear, a new year is aborning;
And so are you, perpet'ually. Gmorning.

Find words for all your daily joys & terrors.
Gnight; make work that gets us in our feelings.
Send off to bed your doubt, your shame, your errors;
Break curfew with your muses, shatter ceilings.
The year is fresh; wipe clean inertia's mildew.
Grateful for all you do, & all you will do.

Gmorning!
Yikes, I almost attempted the gmorning
without coffee and a shower.
Take CARE of yourself before leaping into
the world. Take CARE! Love you!

Gnight!
Almost went to bed while reading the news.
Give yourself a minute before you fall asleep;
get your mind right! Love you!

Good morning.
Don't wait on anyone to make your favorite thing.
Make your own favorite thing.
Go.

Good night.
Don't let anyone set parameters on your dreams.
Your dreams are yours
and yours alone.
Go.

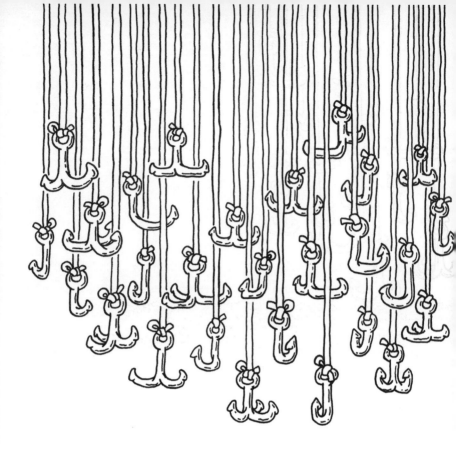

Good morning.
Do NOT get stuck in the comments section of life today.
Make, do, create the things.
Let others tussle it out.
Vamos!

Good night.
Don't let the world's clickbait pull you off your path.
Unplug, explore, dream new terrain.
The world keeps spinning.
A dormir!

Good morning, you.

Yes, you.

YOU RIGHT THERE, LOOKIN' CUTE AS YOU WANNA BE.

Damn, you gon' knock 'em out today! Go!

Good night, you.

Yes, you.

You there, LOOKIN' FRESH AS HELL.

Check you out.

Leavin' a trail of people dreaming about you in your wake.

Gmorning.
Unclench your fists.
Lower your shoulders.
Step away.
Then come back with a clear head,
redouble your efforts.
I believe in you.

Gnight.
Unclench your fists.
Lower your shoulders.
Step away.
Come back with a clear head *mañana,*
redouble your efforts.
I believe in you.

Good morning.
I know it seems like everyone left
without you for the party,
and those stepsisters suck,
but us woodland creatures are on your side.

Good night.
I know it seems like everyone is at the Prince's ball
all the time,
but it's okay to go home before midnight.
Kick off your shoes.

Good morning.
If we're picking teams,
I call dibs on you.
Thanks for being around.

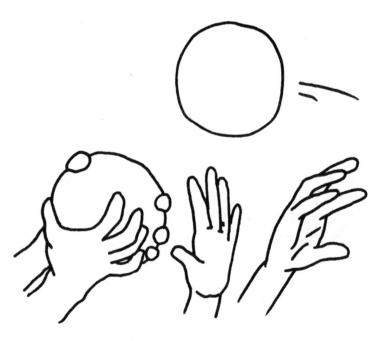

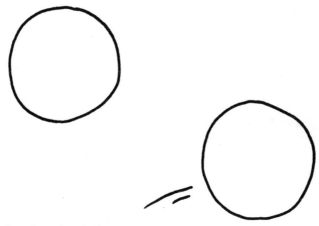

Good night.
Great team, great game.
You are CLUTCH!

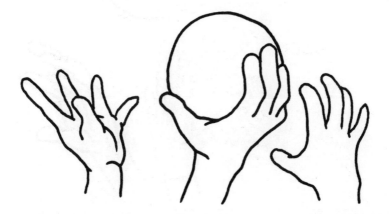

Good morning, people of every color, shape, and stripe! Hold up: you with the stripes, get over here, that's awesome!

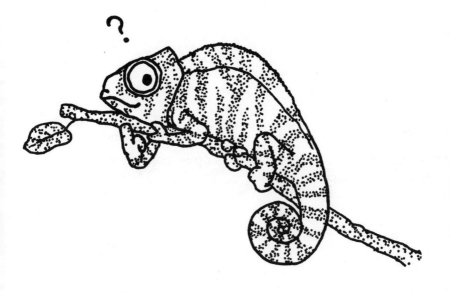

Good night, people of every shape, color, and stripe.
And those of you who change colors in the sun.

Gmorning.
Allow for the possibility that
the best of you is still inside
you, waiting to emerge.
Prepare the way,
bit by bit.

Gnight.
Allow for the possibility that
the best stuff is still ahead of
you, waiting to reveal itself.
Prepare the way,
bit by bit.

Good morning!
You are the bees' knees!
The lambs' gams!
The calves' calves!
Bethenny Frankel's ankles!
Invent new idioms!
Let's go!

Good night!
You're the cream in my coffee!
The sugar in my bowl!
The absinthe in my cocktail!
The syrup in my Slurpee!
Tasty dreams, let's go!

Good morning.
Words fail us, often, but when we put 'em together the
right way they can pull boulders out of us.
Keep working with 'em.

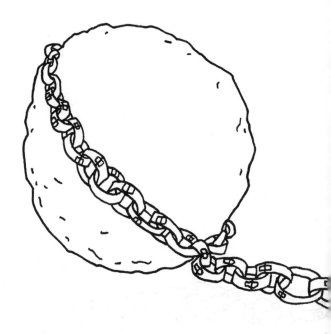

Good night.

Tomorrow we take pen to pad, move mountains.

Get some rest.

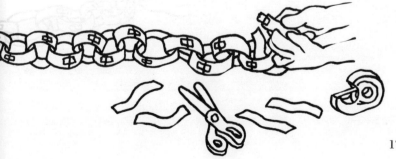

Good morning.
It's okay to let your mind drift.
Whoa, cool drift, kid!

Good night.
So glad we're drift compatible.

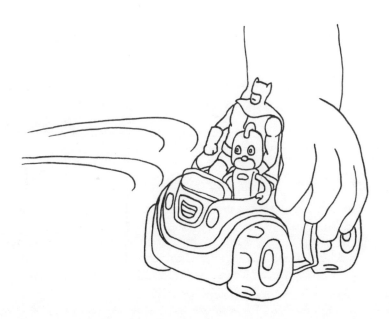

Gmorning.
You're stunning and the world is
lucky to have you.
We are LUCKY TO HAVE YOU.
Do your best.

Gnight.
You're stunning and the world is
lucky to have you.
We are LUCKY TO HAVE YOU.
Get some rest.

Good morning.
Give a little more than you think you can today.
It'll come back around somehow, I promise.
That's what I got for you.

Good night.
New ideas are waiting for you on
the other side of sleep.
Don't be afraid of going to meet 'em.
Yeah? Yeah.

Gmorning.

Subways may be slow.

Traffic may crawl to a halt.

Still, you're on your way.

You are not defined by the speed of your surroundings.

Your mind is racing.

You're on your way, damnit.

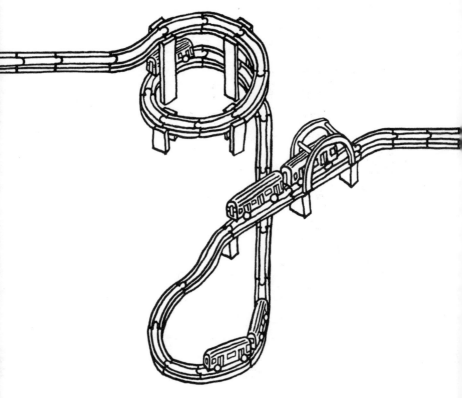

Gnight.
Days may be slow.
You may face setbacks.
Still, you're on your way.
Your tempo is not dictated by your surroundings.
Your heartbeat is your own.
You're on your way, damnit.

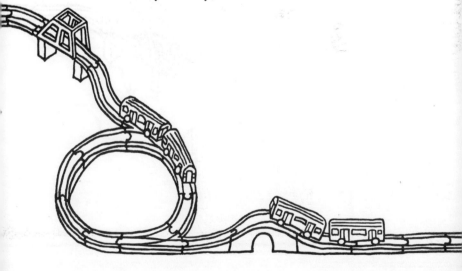

Gmorning.
Try and face the world with
your best self, even if the world
doesn't respond in kind.
Don't do them, do you.

Gnight.
Tomorrow we try again.
Rest up.

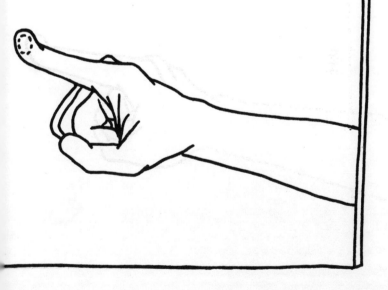

Good morning.
Courage.
Even when the panic's at the back of your throat,
courage.
Let's go.

Good night.
Courage.
Even when fear is at the foot of your bed, courage.
Let's go.

Gmorning.
Set the thermostat for your heart today.
The temp where you like it.
You know yourself, you know what you need.
Take your time.

Gnight.
Set the thermostat for your heart tonight.
The temp where you like it.
You know yourself, you know what you need.
Take your time.

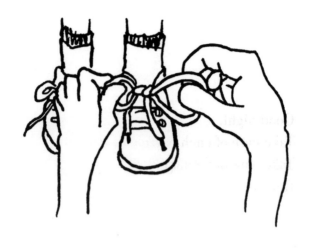

Good morning.
Take care of each other.
Take care of yourself.
Repeat.

Good night.
Take care of each other.
Take care of yourself.
Repeat.

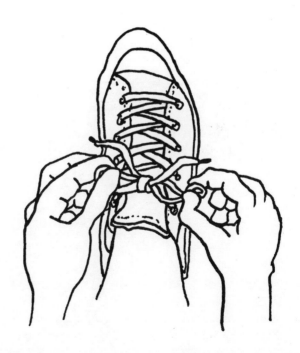

Gmorning.
Look at you!
Damn, you all right!
Pssh. They ain't ready for you!

Gnight.
Dag, check you out!
Told you they weren't ready.
Rest all that greatness!

Good morning.
You will have to say no to things to say yes
to your work.
It will be worth it.

Good night.
Don't forget to look up from your work &
let real life in.
It makes your work better.

Gmorning.
Get out of your own head for a sec.
Do something good today for someone else.
They'll appreciate it
(and so will your head).

Gnight.
Climb back into your own head for a sec.
Take stock of what you've got, and what
you need.
You'll appreciate it
(and so will your head).

Good morning.
You are perfectly cast in your life.
I can't imagine anyone but you in the role.
Go play.

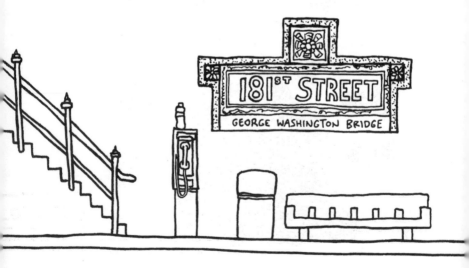

Good night.
You are perfectly cast in your life.
And with so little rehearsal too!
It's a joy to watch. Thank you.

Gmorning.
Pain, joy, frustration, euphoria, everything.
It all passes. It all keeps moving.
Wherever you are is temporary.
Let's go!

Gnight.
Rage, bliss, fatigue, rapture, everything.
It all passes. It all keeps moving.
Where you are is fleeting.
Andiamo.

Gmorning.
Tired, but grateful.
Sick, but grateful.
It's grey out, but I'm grateful.
So much easier to start with grateful.

Gnight.
Tired, but grateful.
Sick, but grateful.
It's dark out, but I'm grateful.
So much easier to end with grateful.

acknowledgements

Lin-Manuel & Jonny would like you to know that this book wouldn't exist without everyone we talk to all day on Twitter (Twitterico, affectionately), and also Kassandra Tidland; Ben Greenberg; John Buzzetti & Andy McNicol at WME; Daniel Greenberg & Tim Wojcik at LGR Literary; designer Simon Sullivan; Sarah Kay in the group text; *My Neighbor Totoro,* the dad from *My Neighbor Totoro;* Vanessa Nadal; Elissa Caccavella; Sebastian, Francisco, & Tobillo Miranda; Christopher Sun; the Suns and the Caccavellas; and the sun for giving us gmornings/gnights.

about the authors

LIN-MANUEL MIRANDA is an award-winning composer, lyricist, and performer, as well as the recipient of a 2015 MacArthur Foundation Award. His current musical, *Hamilton*—book, music, and lyrics by Miranda; he also originated the title role—opened on Broadway in 2015. *Hamilton* was awarded the 2016 Pulitzer Prize for Drama and earned a record-breaking sixteen Tony Award nominations, winning eleven Tonys, including two for Miranda personally for Best Book and Best Score of a Musical. Miranda's first Broadway musical, *In the Heights,* received four 2008 Tony Awards (including Best Orchestrations, Best Choreography, and Best Musical). Miranda contributed music, lyrics, and vocals to several songs in Disney's feature film *Moana,* earning him an Oscar nomination and a Grammy Award for the original song "How Far I'll Go." He stars alongside Emily Blunt in Disney's *Mary Poppins Returns.*
He lives in New York City with his wife, sons, and dog.

linmanuel.com
Twitter: @lin_manuel

JONNY SUN is the author and illustrator of *everyone's a aliebn when ur a aliebn too* (Harper Perennial, 2017). Tweeting as @jonnysun, he was named one of *Time* magazine's 25 Most Influential People on the Internet in 2017. He is currently a doctoral candidate at MIT, an affiliate at the Berkman Klein Center for Internet and Society at Harvard University, and a creative researcher for metaLAB at Harvard, where he studies virtual place and online humor. As a playwright, Sun has seen his work performed at the Yale School of Drama and Factory Theatre and Hart House Theatre in Toronto. He previously studied as an architect (M.Arch., Yale) and an engineer (B.A.Sc, University of Toronto). Sun is also the creator of @ tinycarebot and co-creator of the MIT Humor Series. His comedic work has appeared in *Time* magazine, *Buzzfeed*, *Playboy*, *GQ*, and *McSweeney's*, and he has been profiled on NPR and in *The New York Times Magazine*.

jomnysun.com
Twitter: @jonnysun
Instagram: @jonnysun

about the type

This book was set in Bodoni Book, a typeface
named after Giambattista Bodoni (1740–1813),
an Italian printer and type designer. It is not
actually one of Bodoni's fonts but a modern
version based on his style and manner and is
distinguished by a marked contrast between the
thick and thin elements of the letters.